·Eight Concert Duets·

1
Allegro Con Moto

J. BEACH CRAGUN

Allegro con moto

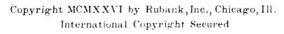

Copyright MCMXXVI by Rubank, Inc., Chicago, Ill.
International Copyright Secured

2
Grazioso

Grazioso

3
Presto

8

4
Largo

Largo

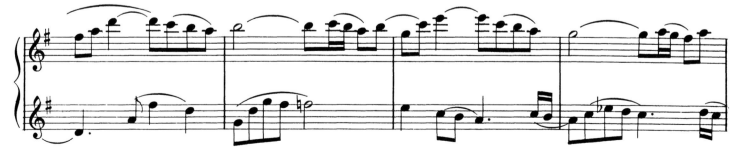

5
Allegro Risoluto

6
Presto Assai

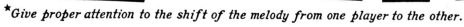

*Give proper attention to the shift of the melody from one player to the other.

7
Moderato

Moderato

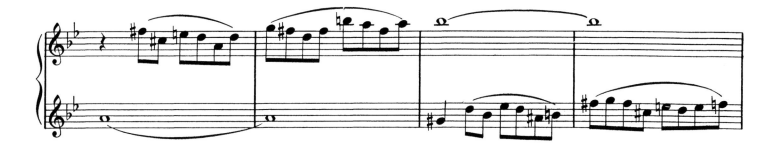

8
Allegro Brillante